TO

My Grandson Finley

FROM

Granpa Stephens

DATE

Sixth Birthday May 9, 2013

Grandpas Are Special People

Artwork by
Susan Winget

HARVEST HOUSE PUBLISHERS
EUGENE, OREGON

Design and production by Garborg Design Works, Savage, Minnesota

GRANDPAS ARE SPECIAL PEOPLE
Copyright © 2011 by Harvest House Publishers
Eugene, Oregon 97402
www.harvesthousepublishers.com
ISBN 978-0-7369-3848-8

The artwork of Susan Winget © is used by Harvest House Publishers, Inc. under authorization from Courtney Davis, Inc. For more information regarding art prints featured in this book, please contact:

>Courtney Davis, Inc.
>55 Francisco Street, Suite 450
>San Francisco, CA 94113
>www.susanwinget.com

Harvest House Publishers has made every effort to trace the ownership of all poems and quotes. In the event of a question arising from the use of a poem or quote, we regret any error made and will be pleased to make the necessary correction in future editions of this book.

Printed in China

11 12 13 14 15 16 17 18 19 / IM / 10 9 8 7 6 5 4 3 2 1

Grandpas are special people because they are...

Grandpa, I like to place my hand in yours.
It makes me feel so safe.

He is the greatest whose strength carries up
the most hearts by the attraction of his own.

HENRY WARD BEECHER

STRONG

Grandpas are special people. They are sure and loving as they scoop up their favorite little ones and give hearty bear hugs to growing grandchildren over the years. Without a second thought, grandpas will transport a sleeping four-year old, a diaper bag, and a life-size purple bear won at the county fair from the car to the upstairs bedroom.

A grandpa knows how to firmly and gently lead his family through all of life's trials and milestones. Everyone knows that they can turn to Grandpa when they need advice, a solid path, and the peace of a strong presence when words are unnecessary.

And when a child needs a lift to reach the top shelf where the best cookies are kept or to gather the hope of heaven, it is Grandpa's strength they depend on.

The heart of a good man

*Life is made up, not of
great sacrifices or duties,
but of little things in which
smiles, and kindnesses,
and small obligations,
given habitually, are what
win and preserve the heart
and secure comfort.*

SIR HUMPHRY DAVY

WHAT IS
STRENGTH
WITHOUT A
DOUBLE SHARE
OF WISDOM?

JOHN MILTON

is the sanctuary of God in this world.

MADAME NECKER

In life we shall find many men that are great, and some men that are good, but very few men that are both great and good.

CHARLES CALEB COLTON

GOODNESS CONSISTS NOT IN THE OUTWARD THINGS WE DO, BUT IN THE INWARD THING WE ARE. TO BE GOOD IS THE GREAT THING.

E.H. CHAPIN

Sincerity, a deep, genuine, heart-felt sincerity, is a trait of true and noble manhood.

LAURENCE STERNE

IT IS NOT WHAT HE HAS, OR EVEN WHAT HE DOES WHICH EXPRESSES THE WORTH OF A MAN, BUT WHAT HE IS.

HENRI-FRÉDÉRIC AMIEL

Six things are requisite to create a "happy home." Integrity must be the architect, and tidiness the upholsterer. It must be warmed by affection, lighted up with cheerfulness; and industry must be the ventilator, renewing the atmosphere and bringing in fresh salubrity day by day; while over all, as a protecting canopy and glory, nothing will suffice except the blessing of God.

ALEXANDER HAMILTON

Where we love is home—home that our feet may leave, but not our hearts.

OLIVER WENDELL HOLMES SR.

Grandpa, you are so special
because you believe in me.

Write your name in kindness, love, and mercy on the hearts of thousands
you come in contact with year by year, and you will never be forgotten.
Your name and your good deeds will shine as the stars of heaven.

ALLAN K. CHALMERS

ENCOURAGING

At the piano recital or the soccer game, the source of the loudest clap and the proudest cheer is always a grandpa. He smiles broadly as he points the camera to capture each once-in-a-lifetime moment. Before he leaves the stands, he gladly announces which child prodigy is of his lineage.

A grandpa understands what it takes to build a forever relationship. He encourages the interests and special gifts of his grandkids by cheering them on. The ears of every grandchild eagerly absorb the encouraging words a grandfather offers during dinner-table conversations or the quiet exchanges they have while picking ruby-red garden tomatoes. And a grandpa's "I love you" echoes forever in a child's heart.

"I know the plans I have for you," declares the LORD, "plans to prosper you and not to harm you, plans to give you hope and a future."

THE BOOK OF JEREMIAH

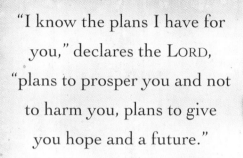

Ye who are old, remember youth with thought of like affection.

WILLIAM SHAKESPEARE

Oh, the joy of young ideas painted on the mind, in the warm, glowing colors fancy spreads on objects not yet known, when all is new and all is lovely!

HANNAH MORE

Words of praise, indeed, are almost as necessary to warm a child into a congenial life as acts of kindness and affection. Judicious praise is to children what the sun is to flowers.

CHRISTIAN NESTELL BOVEE

I LOVE THESE LITTLE PEOPLE; AND IT IS NOT A SLIGHT THING, WHEN THEY WHO ARE SO FRESH FROM GOD, LOVE US.

CHARLES DICKENS

A good deed is never lost.
He who sows courtesy,
reaps friendship; he who
plants kindness, gathers
love; pleasure bestowed
upon a grateful mind
was never sterile, but
generally gratitude
begets reward.

SAINT BASIL

Don't judge each day by the

YOU WILL FIND
AS YOU LOOK
BACK UPON
LIFE THAT
THE MOMENTS
WHEN YOU
HAVE REALLY
LIVED ARE
THE MOMENTS
WHEN YOU
HAVE DONE
THINGS IN
THE SPIRIT
OF LOVE.

HENRY DRUMMOND

This fond attachment to the well-known place
Whence first we started into life's long race,
Maintains its hold with such unfailing sway,
We feel it e'en in age, and at our latest day.

WILLIAM COWPER

harvest you reap, but by the seeds you plant.

ROBERT LOUIS STEVENSON

Grandpa, thank you for being so patient
when I'm trying something new.

In early childhood you may lay the foundation of poverty or riches, industry or idleness, good or evil, by the habits to which you train your children. Teach them right habits then, and their future life is safe.

LYDIA SIGOURNEY

PATIENT

A grandpa loves to walk the same stretch of park again and again with a curious toddler. He pays rapt attention to the fourth explanation of how to make a mud pie and will spend all afternoon piecing together a multilevel dollhouse.

Grandfathers are able to multitask in the most important ways. While they are fixing the faucet, measuring a board, or watching the night sky for a shooting star, they don't shoo away conversations with an impatient sigh. They invite grandkids to explore, participate, and question.

A grandpa extends patience to everyone he meets. He'll chat to the shy boy at the lemonade stand, and he'll offer a reassuring nod to the harried clerk at the checkout line. A granddad will wait for the weather to clear to take his grandson to the best fishing spot, and he'll open up his granddaughter's favorite storybook every evening with a look of delighted anticipation. Best of all, a grandpa waits patiently for those he loves to become the very best they can be.

The king-becoming
graces are justice, verity,
temperance, stableness,
bounty, perseverance,
mercy, lowliness, devotion,
patience, courage, fortitude.

WILLIAM SHAKESPEARE

OUR SWEETEST
EXPERIENCES OF
AFFECTION ARE
MEANT TO POINT
US TO THAT
REALM WHICH IS
THE REAL AND
ENDLESS HOME
OF THE HEART.

HENRY WARD BEECHER

You aspire to great things? Begin with little ones.

SAINT AUGUSTINE

God sends children for another purpose than merely to keep up the race—to enlarge our hearts; and to make us unselfish and full of kindly sympathies and affections; to give our souls higher aims; to call out all our faculties to extended enterprise and exertion; and to bring round our firesides bright faces, happy smiles, and loving, tender hearts.

MARY HOWITT

Grandpa, I love reaching for the sky
when you put me on your shoulders.

Grandchildren don't stay young forever, which is good because Pop-pops have only so many horsey rides in them.

GENE PERRET

FUN

"That reminds me of a time when…" is a grandpa's lead-in to an entertaining story. Grandkids and grandpas share in the fun of blending imagination and experience to create an engaging tale. Maybe that's why they get along so well and laugh together so much.

Every child knows that the only GPS they can count on for fun is Grandpa's Playtime Satellite. From anywhere in town, he can locate the most delicious pepperoni pizza by the slice, a movie theater with good seats for the under-four-foot crowd, and the location of the water park with the most slides.

On some days, Grandpa's best advice is for the family to enjoy the comforts of home. If he spots a blanket and two chairs, he sees the makings of a fort. With a wink and a grin he creates a perfect afternoon out of nothing. A grandpa knows that life is precious, and when the fun begins, he reminds his family of this truth in memorable ways.

NEVER FEAR SPOILING CHILDREN BY
MAKING THEM TOO HAPPY. HAPPINESS
IS THE ATMOSPHERE IN WHICH ALL
GOOD AFFECTIONS GROW.

THOMAS BRAY

Fond Memory brings the light
Of other days around me:
The smiles, the tears
Of boyhood's years.

THOMAS MOORE

Blessed be the hand that prepares a
pleasure for a child, for there is no saying
when and where it may bloom forth.

DOUGLAS JERROLD

Who is not attracted by bright and pleasant children, to prattle, to creep, and to play with them?

EPICTETUS

FUN GIVES YOU A FORCIBLE HUG, AND SHAKES LAUGHTER OUT OF YOU, WHETHER YOU WILL OR NO.

DAVID GARRICK

Teach us delight in simple things.

RUDYARD KIPLING

A good laugh is sunshine in a house.

WILLIAM MAKEPEACE THACKERAY

The cheerful live longest in years, and afterwards in our regards. Cheerfulness is the off-shoot of goodness.

CHRISTIAN NESTELL BOVEE

I like the laughter that opens the lips and the heart, that shows at the same time pearls and the soul.

VICTOR HUGO

Grandpa, you are special because you
always help a neighbor or a stranger in need.

*There never was any heart truly great and gracious
that was not also tender and compassionate.*

ROBERT SOUTH

GIVING

With helping hands and a ready spirit, a grandpa gives to his grandchildren. If a school project deadline is fast approaching, he gathers his tools and helps shape a child's ideas into three-dimensional creations. When a babysitter is needed, he is ready and willing to give his time and his best horsey rides, complete with neigh-neigh sounds, around the living room all evening.

Grandpa possesses a glad and gracious heart. He leads the way through the life experience with courage, integrity, and faith. When the family comes to the table, they look forward to hearing Grandpa say a blessing over the shared meal and their shared lives. His prayers, just like his offerings of help and guidance, are a reminder of his unconditional love.

A grandpa's legacy of compassion, strength, and godly devotion provides his family with an example of what it means to give and live from the heart.

Charity sees the need, not the cause.

GERMAN PROVERB

If God has taught us all truth in teaching

us to love, then he has given us an

interpretation of our whole duty to our

households. We are not born as the partridge

in the wood, or the ostrich of the desert, to be

scattered everywhere; but we are to be grouped

together, and brooded by love, and reared day

by day in that first of churches, the family.

HENRY WARD BEECHER

PHILANTHROPY,
LIKE CHARITY,
MUST BEGIN AT
HOME; FROM
THIS CENTRE
OUR SYMPATHIES
SHOULD EXTEND
IN AN EVER
WIDENING CIRCLE.

CHARLES LAMB

There are three requisites to the proper enjoyment of earthly blessings: a thankful reflection on the goodness of the giver; a deep sense of our own unworthiness; and a recollection of the uncertainty of our long possessing them. The first will make us grateful; the second, humble; and the third, moderate.

HANNAH MORE

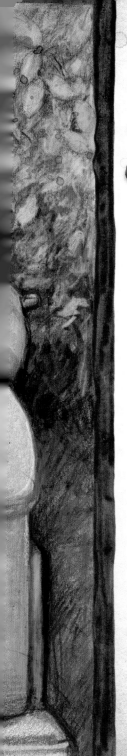

He prayeth best who loveth best.

SAMUEL TAYLOR COLERIDGE

The generous who is always just, and the just who is always generous, may unannounced, approach the throne of heaven.

JOHANN LAVATER

All my experience of the world teaches me that in ninety-nine cases out of a hundred, the safe and just side of a question is the generous and merciful side.

ANNA JAMESON

Grandpa, I love it when you share about your childhood and your family. It reminds me that you and I are part of the same heritage.

Hereditary honors are a noble and
splendid treasure to descendants.

PLATO

HONORABLE

Grandpas are special people who inspire the best in others. They provide the encouraging nudge in the right direction when a child loses his way, and a grandpa gives a pat on the back when a grandchild does a good deed. His generosity and hospitality extend beyond the family. He is known for giving freely of his resources, his time, and his famous grilled burgers to anyone in need of help, fellowship, or a satisfying meal.

A grandpa leads a child on a path toward honor. In all that he does and is, a grandpa shows little ones how to be a part of a family and treat everyone with respect, including themselves. His way of life is a treasure given to his family and also to those he encounters. Each person knows, after meeting Grandpa, that they've witnessed a man of honor who inspires them to live with integrity and kindness.

LIKE A MORNING DREAM, LIFE BECOMES MORE AND
MORE BRIGHT THE LONGER WE LIVE, AND THE REASON OF
EVERYTHING APPEARS MORE CLEAR. WHAT HAS PUZZLED
US BEFORE SEEMS LESS MYSTERIOUS, AND THE CROOKED
PATHS LOOK STRAIGHTER AS WE APPROACH THE END.

JEAN PAUL RICHTER

"There is nothing," says Plato, "So delightful as the hearing or the speaking of truth"—for this reason there is no conversation so agreeable as that of the man of integrity, who hears without any intention to betray, and speaks without any intention to deceive.

JOSEPH ADDISON

Our own heart, and not other men's opinion, forms our true honor.

SAMUEL TAYLOR COLERIDGE

Moral courage is a virtue of higher cast and nobler origin than physical. It springs from a consciousness of virtue, and renders a man, in the pursuit or defense of right, superior to the fear of reproach, opposition, or contempt.

S.G. GOODRICH

His daily prayer, far better understood in acts

A good name is rather to be chosen than great riches, and loving favor rather than silver and gold.

SOLOMON

LET US NEVER FORGET THAT EVERY STATION IN LIFE IS NECESSARY; THAT EACH DESERVES OUR RESPECT, THAT NOT THE STATION ITSELF, BUT THE WORTHY FULFILLMENT OF ITS DUTIES DOES HONOR TO THE MAN.

MARY LYON

than in words, was simply doing good.

JOHN GREENLEAF WHITTIER

True wisdom is to know what is best worth knowing, and to do what is best worth doing.

EDWARD PORTER HUMPHREY

Grandpa, you teach me the
important things like how to whistle!

TEACHERS

When Grandpa is their teacher, grandkids can't wait to learn. A visit to his house is a visit to a classroom of fun life lessons. The great questions of the universe won't trip up Grandpa because he takes the time to unravel whatever needs it…knotted tennis shoes or the mysteries of God. Whatever a grandchild needs becomes a grandfather's area of expertise

A grandpa is also a very quick study. He'll research everything from baseball cards to bubble-gum flavors because he wants to keep the conversation going and express fascination in each child's latest passion. If a child hasn't yet discovered a dream to pursue, a grandfather knows how to inspire a sense of possibility and delight.

Every corner turned, every bump in the road is an opportunity to gather a bit of Grandpa's wisdom. He explains how the sun directs him west and how a flat tire can be fixed in a jiff. And he knows about the really important things—like how to build the ultimate chocolate sundae.

YOU CANNOT
TEACH A
CHILD TO
TAKE CARE
OF HIMSELF
UNLESS YOU
WILL LET
HIM TRY TO
TAKE CARE OF
HIMSELF. HE
WILL MAKE
MISTAKES; AND
OUT OF THESE
MISTAKES
WILL COME
HIS WISDOM.

HENRY WARD BEECHER

Knowledge once gained
casts a light beyond its own
immediate boundaries.

JOHN TYNDALL

Show me your ways, O Lord, teach me your
paths; guide me in your truth and teach me.

THE BOOK OF PSALMS

It is not more wealth
that the world wants, a
thousandth part as much
as it is more character;
not more investments, but
more integrity; not money,
but manhood; not regal
palaces, but regal souls.

E.G. BECKWITH

A man cannot leave a better legacy to the world than a well-educated family.

THOMAS SCOTT

FAMILY EDUCATION
AND ORDER ARE
SOME OF THE
CHIEF MEANS
OF GRACE; IF
THESE ARE DULY
MAINTAINED, ALL
THE MEANS OF
GRACE ARE LIKELY
TO PROSPER
AND BECOME
EFFECTUAL.

JONATHAN EDWARDS

The training of children is a profession, where we must know how to lose time in order to gain it.

JEAN-JACQUES ROUSSEAU

To make knowledge valuable, you must have the cheerfulness of wisdom. Goodness smiles to the last.

RALPH WALDO EMERSON

43

Grandpa, you are the
hero of my heart.

Every man is a volume, if you know how to read him.

WILLIAM ELLERY CHANNING

ONE OF A KIND

There is nobody like Grandpa. His laugh is infectious and so unique that you can actually single it out at the annual family potluck. When he reads bedtime stories and does all the voices—even those of princesses and forest animals—he is giving his grandchild the whole world in a memorable moment that no one else can duplicate.

When little ones are sleepy, they like to lean into the special, made-just-right nook between Grandpa's arm and his chest. Here they will settle into a naptime of happy dreams. They know that Grandpa is their refuge in the storm, whether the rocky winds are from an ongoing trial or a demanding day of finger-painting.

Those who know Granddad seek his solid understanding of what truly matters. His belief in the values of compassion and goodness creates a refuge that extends far beyond the reach of his arms; and yet, it is felt most deeply in the security of his embrace.

THE HIGHEST
MANHOOD
RESIDES IN
DISPOSITION,
NOT IN MERE
INTELLECT.

HENRY WARD BEECHER

The truest greatness lies in being kind,
the truest wisdom in a happy mind.

ELLA WHEELER WILCOX

Perhaps a gentleman is a rarer man than some of us think for. Which of us can point out many such in his circle; men whose aims are generous, whose truth is not only constant in its kind, but elevated in its degree; whose want of meanness makes them simple, who can look the world honestly in the face with an equal manly sympathy for the great and the small?

WILLIAM MAKEPEACE THACKERAY

A HAPPY FAMILY IS BUT AN EARLIER HEAVEN.

JOHN BOWRING

The creed of the true saint is to make the most of life, and to make the best of it.

E.H. CHAPIN

There's a whole lot of folks looking around
Wondering where the greatest man can be found.
Someone worthy of honor and love
Who gathers and gives strength from above.
Well, there's no need to search anymore
Because I know the one they're looking for.
The only man who comes to mind
Is you, Grandpa…you are one of a kind!